Samantha Smith
Young Ambassador

Patricia Stone Martin

illustrated by Bernard Doctor

Rourke Enterprises Vero Beach, Florida

Manufactured in the United States of America

Library of Congress Cataloging-in-Publication Data

Martin, Patricia Stone.
　Samantha Smith – young ambassador

　(Reaching your goal biographies)
　Summary: A biography of the young girl who, as a
result of a letter written to Soviet leader Yuri Andropov,
visited the Soviet Union as an ambassador of peace.
Includes advice on setting and reaching goals.
　1. Smith, Samantha – Juvenile literature. 2. Smith,
Samantha – Journeys – Soviet Union – Juvenile literature.
3. Maine – Biography. 4. Children – United States –
Biography – Juvenile literature. 5. United States –
Relations – Soviet Union – Juvenile literature. 6. Soviet
Union – Relations – United States – Juvenile literature.
[1. Smith, Samantha. 2. Children – Biography. 3. United
States – Relations – Soviet Union. 4. Soviet Union –
Relations – United States] I. Title. II. Series:
Martin, Patricia Stone. Reaching your goal biographies.
CT275.S552M37 1987 973.927′092′4 [B] [92] 87-12127
ISBN 0-86592-173-3

Ten-year-old Samantha Smith sat close to her TV set. The man on the screen talked about war. Samantha did not like that. Did Russia want to fight our country?

She decided to write to someone about it. She chose Yuri Andropov. Mr. Andropov was one of the leaders of the Soviet Union. In her letter, she asked him if the Russians wanted war.

Mr. Andropov wrote back to Samantha. He said she was a brave and honest girl. No, he said, Russia did not want war. He invited Samantha to visit his country.

Writing that letter made Samantha famous. Everyone wanted to know more about her: She became a young ambassador. An ambassador is someone who speaks for his or her country.

Samantha Smith was born on June 29, 1972, in Houlton, Maine. The Smiths moved to Manchester, Maine, when Samantha was in the third grade.

Samantha wrote her letter in November of 1982. She was in the fifth grade. The next spring she got a letter from Mr. Andropov. She had almost forgotten that she wrote to him.

People began to call Samantha. She was invited to be on TV shows. Even people from other countries called her.

Before she wrote her letter, Samantha was very shy. She would not even try out for the school play. Then suddenly she was on TV talk shows. She quickly learned not to be shy.

One artist even wanted to "paint" a picture of Samantha with jelly beans. Samantha said that was fine with her, if she could eat the picture!

On July 8, 1983, Samantha and her parents went to the Soviet Union. The Soviet Union is the correct name for Russia. Russia is just one part of the Soviet Union. The country is also called the USSR, which stands for Union of Soviet Socialist Republics.

The first city the Smiths visited was Moscow. They stayed in a hotel that looked like a palace. They saw many famous places. They saw a large church with golden domes. The domes looked like big onions.

They went to Crimea, a part of the Soviet Union. Crimea is on the Black Sea. The Black Sea is very salty. Samantha had no trouble floating in such salty water.

The Young Pioneers have a camp there. Boys and girls have to make very good grades to be Young Pioneers. Samantha stayed with the Pioneers at their camp. She talked with them. The Soviet children asked her questions about America. They told Samantha that they did not want war.

The Smiths went to Leningrad next. Leningrad is one of Russia's largest and most beautiful cities. They saw many palaces. Samantha put flowers on monuments.

Then they returned to Moscow. They went to the Moscow Circus and to the Toy Museum. They saw the Animal Theater and the Puppet Theater.

Mr. Andropov sent gifts to Samantha at her hotel. He was very busy while she was in Moscow, so Samantha did not get to meet him.

Samantha enjoyed her trip. She ate good food. She made new friends. She saw new places. Best of all, she found out that boys and girls in Russia are just like boys and girls in America.

When Samantha came home, she wrote a book. She called it *Journey to the Soviet Union*. The book tells all about Samantha's trip. It is filled with beautiful pictures of the Soviet Union and pictures of Samantha, her parents, and her Soviet friends.

The next January, Samantha went to Japan. She talked to children there too. People in Japan called her the "Angel of Peace."

Samantha liked to talk about peace, and she liked to travel. Her father gave up his teaching job to travel with her.

Samantha also liked staying home. She had a dog named Kim. One day Kim had eight puppies. Samantha also owned 20 mice! She wanted to be an animal doctor when she was older.

Samantha talked about her trips and her book on TV talk shows. Robert Wagner, an actor, saw her on the "Tonight Show." He wanted Samantha to play the part of his daughter on a new TV show. The show was "Lime Street." Samantha tried out for the part. She got it!

When she was working in "Lime Street," Samantha had to be away from home. Then she missed her friends. At school, her friends always called her Sam. She missed going to dances and parties with them.

But she loved acting on "Lime Street." She called Mr. Wagner "R.J." Sometimes she made mistakes on her lines. Then she grinned and said them again. Everyone thought she was a good actress.

The fourth show of "Lime Street" was made in England in September of 1985. Samantha's father went to England with her. On the way back home, their plane crashed. The plane was only 30 miles from Samantha's house! All eight people on the plane were killed, including Samantha and her father.

Samantha was only 13 years old when she died. She wanted people to know that peace is important. She wanted us to know that everyone can be friends. Samantha reached her goals. She made people all around the world think about peace.

Reaching Your Goal

What are your goals? Here are some steps to help you reach them.

1. **Decide on your goal.**
   It may be a short-term goal like one of these:
   learning to ride a bike
   getting a good grade on a test
   keeping your room clean
   It may be a long-term goal like one of these:
   learning to read
   learning to play the piano
   becoming a lawyer

2. **Decide if your goal is something you really can do.**
   Do you have the talent you need?
   How can you find out? By trying!
   Will you need special equipment?
   Perhaps you need a piano or ice skates.
   How can you get what you need?
   Ask your teacher or your parents.

3. Decide on the first thing you must do.
Perhaps this will be to take lessons.

4. Decide on the second thing you must do.
Perhaps this will be to practice every day.

5. Start right away.
Stick to your plan until you reach your goal.

6. Keep telling yourself, "I can do it!"

Good luck! Maybe someday you will become an ambassador like Samantha Smith.

Reaching Your Goal Books

Beverly Cleary
She Makes Reading Fun

Bill Cosby Superstar

Jesse Jackson A Rainbow Leader

Ted Kennedy, Jr.
A Lifetime of Challenges

Christa McAuliffe
Reaching for the Stars

Dale Murphy
Baseball's Gentle Giant

Dr. Seuss We Love You

Samantha Smith Young Ambassador

Rourke Enterprises, Inc.
P.O. Box 3328
Vero Beach, FL 32964

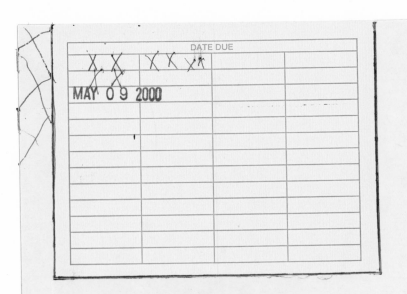

92
SMI

Martin, Patricia
Stone.

Samantha Smith--
young ambassador.

787230   15096D